WHO WANTS TO LEARN WITH ME?

Written By LaTonya D. Steele   Illustrated By Aranahaj Iqbal

Copyright © 2018 by Learning with Harmony, LLC.
www.learningwithharmony.com
Book Cover & Illustrations Designed by
Aranahaj Iqbal

All rights reserved. No part of this book may be reproduced or transmitted in any form or by any means, electronic or mechanical, including photocopying, recording, or by any information storage and retrieval system, without permission in writing from the author.

ISBN-13: 978-1-948398-00-8

About the Author

LaTonya D. Steele has spent 20+ years of her career teaching high school and adult learners business courses in the community college system. She is a firm believer that a good education is essential for all ages. She has a passion for giving back to others and helping them succeed in reaching their academic, professional and personal goals. LaTonya has a Ph.D. in Management and is a lifelong learner.

Since the birth of her first granddaughter, LaTonya has recently developed a new interest in writing educational books for children. She started writing books for her granddaughter and wanted to share them with other children, families, caregivers, and early childhood educators. LaTonya decided to make an educational book series (**Learning with Harmony**) for children from birth to 4 years old. The main characters in the book are her granddaughter Harmony and dog Penny.

About the Illustrator

Aranahaj Iqbal has been illustrating for the last 5 years and has many published books. She enjoys illustrating children's books. She also provides illustrations for book series, single books and long-term projects. You can visit her Facebook page at facebook.com/aranahajart, Instagram at aranahajiqbal and Twitter at Aranahaji (ARANAHAHJI) to see her portfolios.

Hi, my name is Harmony. I like to learn new things to help me grow and develop.

Penny is a brown dog. She is my friend. She helps me learn. Do you have any pets?

I will learn how to talk and read one day.
Can you say, mama?

I will learn how to crawl. Do you know how to get on your hands and knees?

Then, I will learn how to walk. Do you have a favorite pair of shoes?

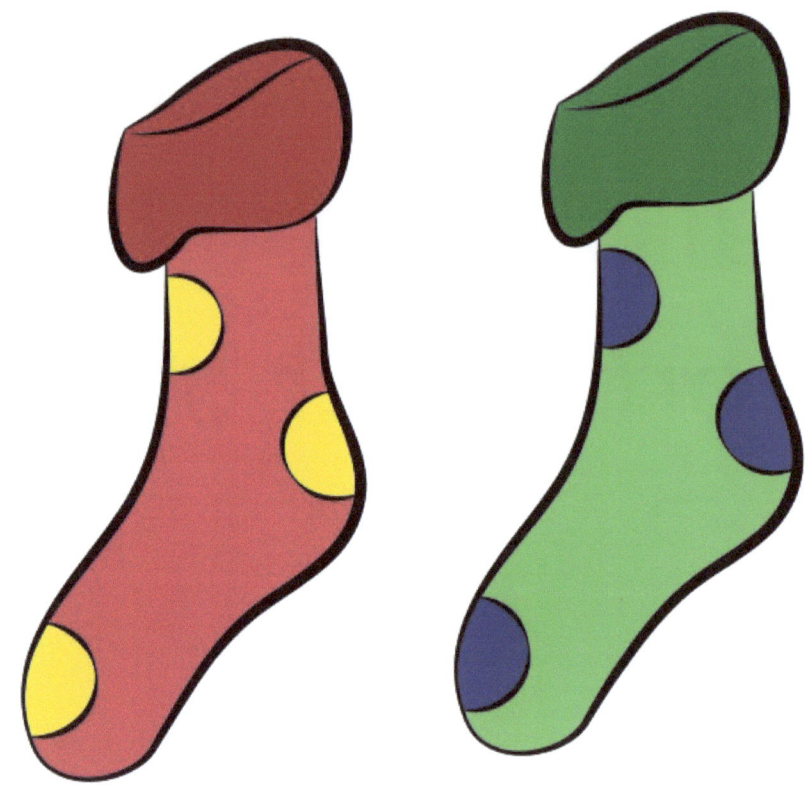

I will learn about colors. Can you help me find my red sock?

I will learn about shapes. Which one is the heart?

I will learn about insects. Please help me find the bumblebee.

I will learn about farm and zoo animals. Do you see the monkey?

I will learn about alphabets. Which one is the letter A?

1 2 3 4 5
6 7 8 9 10

I will learn about numbers. Can you help me find the number 3?

I will learn how to count objects. How many balloons do you see?

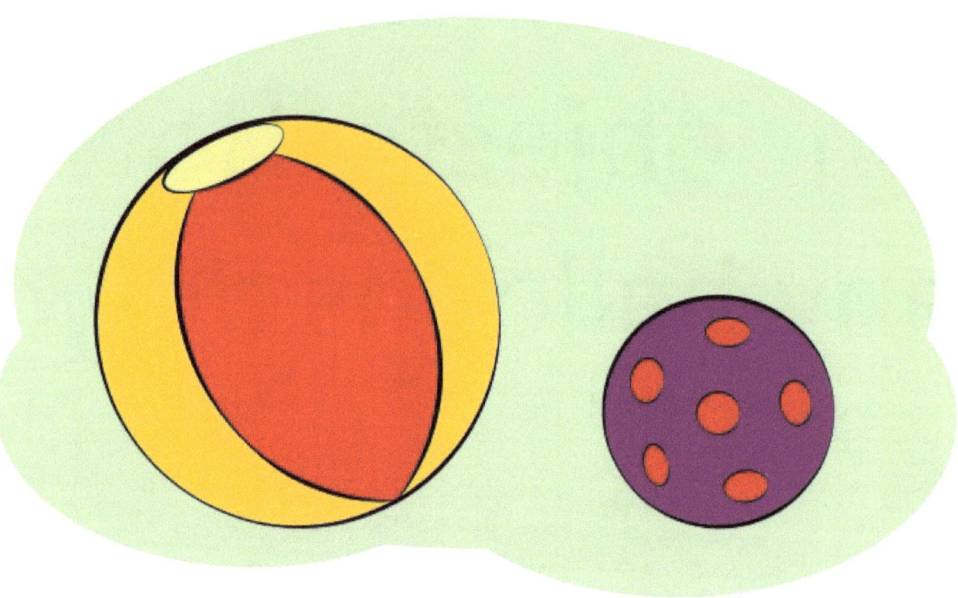

I will learn about opposites. Which one is my small ball?

I have a lot to learn. Reading is going to be fun! Do you want to learn with me?

www.ingramcontent.com/pod-product-compliance
Lightning Source LLC
Chambersburg PA
CBHW041227040426
42444CB00002B/72